Walking in Bowland and Pendle

by
Cyril Spiby
on behalf of the Ramblers' Association
(Mid Lancashire Area)

Dalesman Books
1984

The Dalesman Publishing Company Ltd.,
Clapham, via Lancaster, LA2 8EB

First published 1984
© Ramblers' Association (Mid Lancashire Area) 1984
ISBN: 0 85206 797 6

By the same author:-

Walking in Central Lancashire,	1977 (revised 1980)
Walking in the Ribble Valley,	1977 (revised 1981)

Printed by Swannack Brown & Co. Ltd., Hull, England

Contents

Cover Design by Susan Smith
Maps by Harry Turner

Car Information: All walks are circular to cater for car travellers who have to finish back at the starting point; parking places have been suggested in all cases.

Bus Information: All bus services used are Ribble unless otherwise stated. On walks Nos. 3, 4, 9 and 10 there is the opportunity of travelling on "Betty's Bus", a rural service operated by Ribble. Betty, the driver/conductor, has made the service so unique that it has featured on television; some passengers travel on this bus just for the experience.

Leedham's Bus Service is used for walks Nos. 7, 8, 9, 11 and 12. It operates between Clitheroe railway station and Slaidburn, Monday to Saturday, via Bashall Eaves School, Cow Ark, Whitewell, Dunsop Bridge and Newton.

Departs Clitheroe	0855	1045	1505	1745
Arrives Slaidburn	0945	1135	1555	1835
Departs Slaidburn	0800	0950	1215	1645
Arrives Clitheroe	0850	1040	1305	1735

Foreword

HERE at last is the third book of rambles from the (seemingly tireless) pen of Cyril Spiby. To those who have read and used the previous volumes* I need say only two things: first, the scenery is if anything even more varied and attractive; and secondly, in keeping with the RA policy of encouraging rural transport, Cyril has included more detailed information on bus stops and bus services. There are now a variety of weekly and daily cheap tickets which make rambling by bus or train a more economic proposition today than it was a year or two ago, and we hope that readers will take advantage of this fact.

As in the first two books, the route descriptions have all been tested before publication by a team of human "guinea pigs" and amended wherever necessary. If you follow Cyril's instructions you should have no trouble finding the way, but, as always, we strongly recommend taking the appropriate Ordnance Survey maps with you, "just in case".

This is not a book for the casual stroller, but for the true rambler who is properly equipped and prepared to negotiate trackless country and ford the occasional stream (of which due notice is given in the descriptions!).

Thanks are due to Mr. P K Roberts of Ribble Motors for supplying bus information; to Harry Turner of the Lake District RA for again drawing the maps; to the "guinea pigs" (see above); and last but not least to Betty Spiby for advice, patience and many hours of hard work typing and reading back.

All the walks are new and (to the best of our knowledge) have not been published before. If you have any difficulty of any kind while using the book, please write explaining the problem to Cyril Spiby, 15 Cottam Hall Lane, Ingol, Preston PR2 3XB (enclosing S.A.E.). Telephone 731979 (0772).

**Alan Howard,
Chairman, Ramblers Association (Mid Lancashire Area),
July 1984.**

*Walking in Central Lancashire (1977) and Walking in the Ribble Valley (1978).

1   Easily Overlooked

Whalley via Dean Clough Reservoir: 9 miles.

Short version: 7 miles.

Buses: Whalley has connections with Preston, Blackburn and Clitheroe.

Parking: Leave the main road (King Street) at the traffic lights in the town centre. First turn on the right leads onto the car park (map ref. 734361).

Map O.S. 2½in. Pathfinder Series sheet SD 63/73.

ALTHOUGH well known to Great Harwood walkers, this area is so well hidden that it can be easily overlooked by others. Apart from having its full share of good scenery and excellent viewpoints, this route is useful when fields are waterlogged because much of it is along tracks and minor roads.

Whalley to Great Harwood Cricket Ground: Whether starting from the bus station or car park, turn left along King Street to reach Whalley Bridge over the river Calder. On your right are Whalley Abbey grounds and on your left, Bridge Cottage where Harrison Ainsworth wrote "The Lancashire Witches".

Immediately over the bridge turn left, not along the riverside, but up-hill to a track on the left of the first bend. This worn route climbs Whalley Nab alongside a left-hand boundary to give a grandstand view of the river above the weir(where women accused of being witches were thrown in with their thumbs and toes tied together; if they did not sink immediately it was proof that they were witches).

Continue along the left-hand boundary to reach the top of the climb where Pendle Hill, on your left, is another reminder of witches. From this angle you are looking along its full length, with the summit nearly five miles away. Padiham power station can be seen, with Huncoat power station to its right. Behind the latter is Great Hameldon with the radio tower on Hameldon Hill to its left.

Also at the top of the climb, a track comes in from the right but keep ahead, avoiding other turnings, for ¼ mile. This will bring you to Whalley Banks Farm on your left, identified by ornamental gates bearing its name and an eagle. One hundred yards after this the road bends sharply to the right at a white-painted old farmhouse. A cinder path (sign-posted "Great Harwood") leads off on the left here to reach a storage area after 50 yards. Two paths (running alongside each other at first) continue ahead on the left of the storage area. Choose the right-hand one, a dark sunken way which widens to reach Heys Farm after ⅓rd mile. Ignore a tarmac road that goes off on the

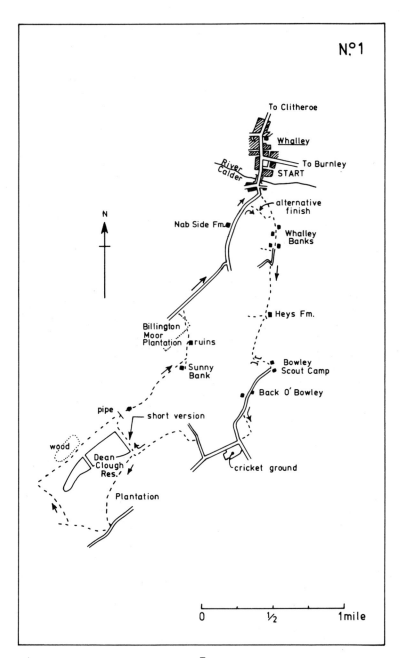

N° 1

To Clitheroe

Whalley

To Burnley

River Calder

START

alternative finish

Nab Side Fm.

Whalley Banks

N

Heys Fm.

Billington Moor Plantation

ruins

Sunny Bank

Bowley Scout Camp

Back O' Bowley

pipe

short version

wood

Dean Clough Res.

cricket ground

Plantation

0   ½   1 mile

right, but turn right just afterwards along a track flanked by walls. Later this descends to cross Dean Bridge then climbs to a junction.

Bowley Scout Camp is to the left, but go right on a tarmac road, to pass dwellings at Back O'Bowley. There is a track on the left of a bend as you climb, but continue along the road for 100 yards to a stile on the left. (Before crossing this, notice the bump on the right-hand side of the road ahead - this is Bowley Hill). Follow a left-hand wall, first through a field then through woodland to join a track. Turn right to reach a road junction.

Great Harwood Cricket Ground to Dean Clough Reservoir: Keep ahead to pass the cricket ground on your left and take the first on the right, Goldacre Lane. At the bottom of the hill a track on the left (signposted "York Road") takes you to Dean Clough Reservoir after ½ mile.

For the **short version,** cross the dam and turn right after a kissing gate, alongside a wire fence to reach a pipe in a hollow. (For continuation see next-but-one paragraph).

For the full walk, keep to the left of the reservoir wall to join an enclosed path after crossing two stiles, and climb for ⅔ mile alongside a plantation to reach the road. Turn right and less than 100 yards along, there is a stile opposite a layby. An interesting grass track angles away from the road, then after a short break, continues at a stiled gateway and passes by three stoops. About 100 yards before reaching the remains of School Lands Farm, turn right at a reedy stream alongside a low ridge. The wall that curves along the top end of the reservoir comes into view and you descend to pass to the left of where this forms an apex. At this point, angle away uphill, to the left, on a green track to meet another track on the nearside of a wall.

Dean Clough Reservoir to Whalley: This track comes back along the other side of the valley, past a wood, to reach a stiled gateway opposite the dam. Ahead is the pipe in the hollow where both versions of the walk converge. Cross the hollow and continue alongside a right-hand wall, then a fence, as you pass the ruins of Fearley Hey. Continue forward through two fields divided by a broken wall, to leave the second at a gap, ignoring a stile in the nearby right-hand corner. Keep above a wooded area with a white house below.

A right-hand wall continues as a guide, then you pass above "Sunny Bank", another house, to cross a right-hand fence near a small quarry. Follow a track uphill through a gateway, to reach some ruins where you turn right to keep outside the enclosure fence to reach a stile in the field corner after bypassing a stile on your right then enter Billington Moor Plantation at the stile ahead.

A few yards inside the plantation, fork right along a vague path which cuts across a corner to reach a stile and wallgap, where you leave the plantation. Incline left uphill to join a road at a rail, after crossing two broken walls on the way. Turn right along this quiet road which runs along the top of Billington Moor, then turn left at a junction (prominent television mast nearby). As you descend into Whalley there are views of the well-known railway viaduct and the abbey ruins close by.

Instead of keeping to the road, there is an optional route which involves climbing a little and puts ⅓rd mile on the walk, but if you have the time it is worthwhile for the views.

About ¼ mile past Nab Side Farm, fork right over a cattle grid and follow an open road which climbs gradually and passes into Nab Wood. When it bends right, take the path which goes back to the left at a row of conifers, and retrace your early route downhill, to the road, and turn right into Whalley.

2   Around Sabden Valley

Spring Wood Picnic Site, Whalley via Sabden Valley: 9½ miles.
Clitheroe/Burnley bus service Nos. 227, 237 and 257.

Car park at the picnic site (map reference 741361), or for an alternative start, Black Hill Picnic Site (map reference 786½ 367½).

Bus users can end the ramble at Sabden (3½ miles) or White Hill crossroads (6¾ miles).

Map O.S. 2½in. Pathfinder Series Sheet SD 63/73.

HOW remote Sabden valley must have been at the time of the Lancashire witches, tucked away as it is with the heights of Read and Padiham on one side, Wiswell Moor on the other, and shielded by the great mass of Pendle Hill. Even today this beautiful valley is relatively isolated and has all the ingredients for a good ramble.

Spring Wood to Nick of Pendle: From the picnic site, turn left to a gap in the wall on the left, after about 50 yards. Climb up the left hand side of Whalley golf-course to leave at a railed footbridge on the left about 20 yards beyond the end of Spring Wood. Continue forward to join and follow a left-hand fence uphill, to a stile in the top corner, from where you can look back at a good view of Whalley and Whalley Nab.

Just around the corner on the right there is another stile, followed by a third also on the right. Here you have a wall on your right which you leave, but rejoin after cutting across a corner. Pass by a garden to join a track. Through a gateway to the right, follow an access road away from "Clerk Hill" to join a minor road where you turn left.

Keep forward at Wiswell Moor Farm and forward again at Wiswell Moor Houses, where the route becomes a grass track, with Pendle ahead and Sabden Valley down to your right. For more than ½ mile you have a wall on your left, then a wall on your right. For a while the track leaves the wall to seek less boggy ground before continuing past Wilkin Heys Farm and the isolated Parsley (Paslew) Barn to reach the road below the Nick of Pendle (bus travellers can walk downhill for ¾ mile to catch a bus at Four Lane Ends, Sabden).

Nick of Pendle to Black Hill Picnic Site: Cross over to continue by a green track just to the right, but after 50/60 yards, leave it to follow a faint narrow path on the right. At first your route is over level but rough ground. When the path fades away, use a plantation backed by Spence Moor (a large section of Pendle Hill) as a marker. Shortly the way descends to a track which leads on to a kissing gate, through which fork right, uphill, to pass to the left of Calf Hill summit. A left-

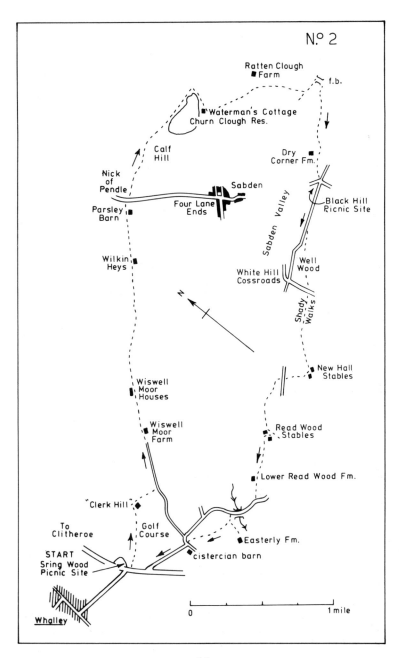

Ratten Clough Farm

f.b.

Waterman's Cottage
Churn Clough Res.

Calf Hill

Dry Corner Fm.

Nick of Pendle

Sabden

Black Hill Picnic Site

Four Lane Ends

Parsley Barn

Sabden Valley

Wilkin Heys

Well Wood

White Hill Cossroads

Shady Walks

N

New Hall Stables

Wiswell Moor Houses

Read Wood Stables

Wiswell Moor Farm

Lower Read Wood Fm.

"Clerk Hill

To Clitheroe

Golf Course

Easterly Fm.

START
Sring Wood
Picnic Site

cistercian barn

0   1 mile

Whalley

11

hand wall leads downhill through a stiled gateway, then you join a track which goes around Churn Clough Reservoir.

Leave this track when you are near the deserted waterman's cottage, by going through a small gate by some railings on the left. Follow the right-hand railings to pass through another small gate in line with the cottage. Bear left in the next field to follow the right-hand boundary through two fields to reach Ratten Clough farm-road. Cross a cattle grid on the right.

Turn left immediately to follow a boundary through three fields, leaving the third at a wall stile on the left. Ford a stream and bear right through a gateway, then continue with the stream and wall on your right. When they bear away, keep forward to cross another stream at a grassy bridge to reach a stile on the left of a gateway. Follow a track to the left to reach a footbridge after about 230 yards, where you cross Sabden Brook (further up the valley you will see Dean Farm, the oldest dated farm [1574] in the valley).

Over the brook, bear right to pass to the right of a section of wall and close in to another wall further back on the left, to cross it at a stile short of where this boundary changes to a fence. Bear right, climbing very gradually as you bear away from the right-hand boundary, then follow a worn path over more level ground, to cross another wall stile. Still keep the same direction, inclining up to pass to the left of an external corner, then follow a right-hand wall. When this bends towards Dry Corner Farm, join a sunken green track that climbs up to join the road at Padiham Heights cross-roads, near Black Hill Picnic Site.

Black Hill Picnic Site to Spring Wood Picnic Site: Take the minor road past the picnic site to reach a stile on the left after ⅓rd mile, where the plantations start. Enter a field at another stile and turn right, alongside the boundary wall of Well Wood and follow the stiles to the road.

A new vista opens up along this stretch; Padiham is down to your left with Hameldon Hill(with wireless mast) beyond, and Great Hameldon to its right.

Bus travellers can go along the road to the right for 300 yards to catch the bus at White Hill cross-roads, but to continue the ramble, take the track opposite, into a wood. Fork right along a path known as Shady Walks, which keeps to the top of a low escarpment and is overgrown in places. On emerging into a field at a wall-stile, keep the same direction along Read Heights, to leave at a stiled gateway in the far left-hand corner.

Turn right along a track, to a wall-stile on the nearside of the first building on the right, belonging to New Hall Stables. A path (that fades) inclines left up a wooded bank to a wall-stile leading into a field. Bear slightly left, then descend, after crossing an unusual cutting, to join a road at a stile opposite the left-hand end of a wood. This road is named "Old Roman Road" on old maps (the cutting is named "Ancient Road"), but another theory is that it was dug in the quest for coal.

A gateway opposite the stile leads into a field, which you leave in the next corner, then bear left over an uneven field to leave at a stile in the diagonal corner. Cross a stile on the right and follow a left-hand fence downhill to enter the yard of Read Wood Stables at a gate. Turn left to join and follow the access road for about 40 yards, then double back along another access road on the right and follow for nearly 100 yards. Near the end of the yard, turn left to follow a track downhill, then across a brook to a stile on the left, over which go forward to cross a fence in a dip just ahead, and ford a stream.

Lower Read Wood Farm is ahead. Pass to the left of the farm and enclosure to join the access road which leads forward past "Brook Side" to reach "Old Roman Road" again. Downhill to the right is Read Old Bridge over Sabden Brook where a decisive battle was fought in 1643. The Earl of Derby had brought an army of 5,000 Royalists from Preston to Whalley. The Parliamentarians could only muster 500, but against the wishes of their commanders, they lay in wait behind the roadside walls. Surprise won the day; the Royalists were completely routed and chased back to Ribchester.

After crossing Read Old Bridge, turn left towards Easterley Farm, another reminder of the battle. Colonel Tyldesley, a Royalist Commander, is said, in his panic, to have mistaken the farm road for the Whalley Road!

About 100 yards along this farm road, cross a stile on the right, then climb directly up a hillside to cross a stiled gateway in the fence at the top. Keep parallel to a left-hand fence as you go downhill, then climb again beyond a stile, keeping to the left of a hollow, then go forward to join the road via a stile.

Your way is forward, downhill, alongside the golf course, then right to Spring Wood Picnic Site, but worthy of note is the Cistercian barn just along to the left. Another interesting item in the field behind the barn is the site of Portfield Iron Age Fort, a raised mound which you can see at the top end of the first field on the left as you start to walk downhill, past the golf course.

3   Moorland in the Sky

Nick of Pendle via Pendle Hill: 10½ miles.

Short version via Mearley Clough: 6½ miles.

The best place for bus travellers to start the ramble is Four Lane Ends, Sabden (map ref. 779375). Burnley - Clitheroe bus service 237/257. From here it is ⅔ mile uphill walk in the direction of Clitheroe to the Nick of Pendle.

Bus travellers also have the choice of finishing at Downham, a total distance of about 8 miles (2 hourly service to Clitheroe).

Parking at the "Nick" (map ref. 772385½).

Maps O.S. 2½in. Sheets SD 63/73, 84/94 (Pathfinder series), and 74.

Map and compass are essential for this ramble.

ABOVE Pendle's steep slopes lies an area of exhilarating moorland which rises to 1831ft, the highest point of any walk in this book. Contrasting with this is the green landscape where the steep slopes merge with the surrounding countryside; these two aspects of Pendle are seen to good effect on this walk.Incidentally, Pendle is triply named as Pen is Celtic for mountain or head, and Holl (now-dle) is Norse for hill. George Fox, founder of the Quakers, climbed it in 1652, only some 4O years after the notorious witches' trial.

Nick of Pendle to Scout cairn: At the highest point of the road between Clitheroe and Sabden, a track goes off on the left opposite the parking area. At first the track takes a fairly level course, then rises to reach the cairn on Apronfull Hill after ¾ mile.

This unusual name is credited to an incident in which the Devil collected an apronful of large stones to bombard Clitheroe Castle (seen below on the left). The Devil's Window in the castle keep is said to be the result of his efforts. It is interesting to note that north-west of Wastwater, there is the name "Samson's Bratful", brat being an old name for an apron.

Ashendean Clough is on your left as you continue to climb steadily for ⅔ mile before gradually descending towards Ogden Clough, the most dramatic of Pendle's many cloughs. Keep it on your right as you bear left on a less distinctive track over broken peat hags until a broken wall is crossed. Here, leave the track and bear left over very rough ground, keeping high to avoid deeper gullies. More than ½ mile beyond the broken wall, there is a cairn which comes into view as you climb. It is well built, with a plaque "75 years of Scouting, 1907-1982" and stands on the edge of the escarpment,looking down left on

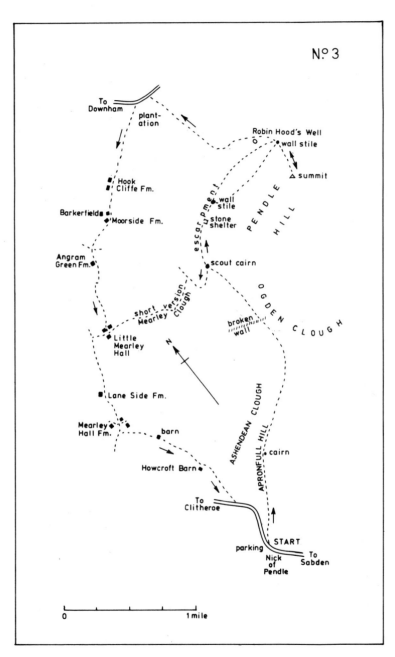

To
Downham

plant-
ation

Robin Hood's Well

wall stile

△ summit

Hook
Cliffe Fm.

wall
stile

Barkerfields

stone
shelter

Moorside Fm.

P E N D L E   H I L L

Angram
Green Fm.

escarpment

scout cairn

O G D E N   C L O U G H

short version
Mearley Clough

broken wall

Little
Mearley
Hall

N

Lane Side Fm.

Mearley
Hall Fm.

barn

A S H E N D E A N   C L O U G H

A P R O N F U L L   H I L L

cairn

Howcroft Barn

To
Clitheroe

START

parking

To
Sabden

Nick
of
Pendle

0   1 mile

steep-sided Mearley Clough. To the right on the horizon is another landmark, a large low wind shelter with stone seats.

Short version, via Little Mearley Hall: Set off south-westerly from the cairn with the clough on your left. You will come to some small cairns and a faint path develops which turns right to avoid a steep stony descent. Choose the best place to leave the path to reach the wall along the bottom of the slope, then follow the wall back to the clough. Your intention now is to follow the clough down, keeping Mearley Brook on your left. There is a rail to cross, adjacent to the brook, then the way is fairly straight-forward through Little Mearley wood ahead to emerge at Little Mearley Hall where the access road leads forward to a junction (see below for continuation).

Little Mearley Hall is a fine example of 16th century architecture; the large bay window is said to have come from Sawley Abbey.

The Scout cairn to Pendle's summit: For the long version, continue along the top of Pendle's escarpment, past the wind shelter (an excellent lunch spot) and cross the wall stile beyond, on the edge of the escarpment. Here you can continue along the escarpment for ¾ mile to reach another wall-stile, or you can cut across to this stile. For this slightly shorter route, bear right along a faint path which starts to bear left a little after approximately 100 yards, and develops into a straight grassy cart-track. This eventually fades when it approaches a prominent gateway in a wall that converges from the right. About 70 yards along the wall to the left, just below the top of the escarpment, is the stile referred to above.

Angle right, beyond the stile, to reach Pendle's summit just over ¼ mile away. Given a clear day, an interesting time can be spent identifying landmarks near and far. Just west of north is flat topped Ingleborough over 20 miles away with Pen-y-ghent to its right. (Note the "Pen").

Pendle's summit to Little Mearley Hall: Retrace your steps and cross the wall stile, then, ignoring a path that follows the wall downhill, follow a faint narrow path that angles downwards and passes "Robin Hood's Well", a copious group of springs (which may entail a detour). After this, the path levels as it contours around Pendle's slope, then angles downhill again before turning directly downhill. A flattish reedy area lies below, which the path crosses directly; about halfway across there is a stiled fence and a stiled wall at the end of the reedy area. Keep forward with a stream and conifer plantation on your left, to reach the road.

Downham is just over a mile to the left by road if you wish to finish there, but to continue the walk, leave the road after 200 yards, where it bends right, by choosing the left-hand of two gateways on the left. At first there is a green enclosed track to follow, alongside the conifer plantation, then a right-hand wall, over which you have a view of Downham Hall, nearly one mile away.

At Hook Cliffe notice the five-light windows with stone mullions and course drip moulds over. (Higher Fairsnape, Bleasale, has similar windows with a datestone of 1637). Pass to the rear and join a concrete farm track where you keep forward past the nearby house. About 100 yards before reaching the next house "Barkerfield", fork left along a green track that climbs to reach a formidable "door" beyond a footbridge. This door, which needs lifting, gives access to Moorside farmyard, through which the farm road leads ahead, with Worsaw Hill away to the right.

At a junction, go through a small gate across to your left, then aim to the left of Angram Green buildings, to cross a stream at a stone slab. Bear left to bypass the farm to reach the external corner of a fenced field, then keep to the right-hand fence and a scant line of hawthorns, to cross a stile in a corner. After crossing a stile 20 yards to the right, turn left to cross a stile by a water trough in the next corner, then leave this field at a gate in the far left-hand corner.

Little Mearley Hall to Nick of Pendle: Follow a right-hand wall and cross a small field, then go forward to reach the far end of Little Mearley Hall farmyard. Turn right to follow the access road already mentioned in the short version, to reach a junction.

Turn left and keep forward at Lane Side Farm along a route lined with holly hedges. At a crossroads, Great Mearley Hall farm is on the right and a creeper covered cottage on the left. Keep forward another 40 yards before turning left between a stream and a fence to cross a stile. Gradually climb for ⅓ mile to reach a barn seen ahead, and pass to the left to discover a stile behind. Beyond, an obvious green track bears right, through a reedy area, but it fades at the top of a rise. Fortunately, your next objective, Howcroft Barn in Ashendean Clough, is now in view. Aided by sheep tracks, aim to the left of it before crossing a well concealed footbridge, opposite the barn end. Ignore a prominent stile as you turn left alongside a wall and follow it around a corner. Gradually angle away from the wall using sheep tracks, as you climb rough ground, keeping the two barns directly in line behind you until the Wellsprings Hotel appears. Turn left and climb up to the Nick of Pendle.

4   **Below Pendle**

Barley via Rimington: 9½ miles.

Short version via Four Lane Ends: 4¼ miles.

Another alternative for bus travellers is to do only half the walk, i.e. start at Barley and finish at the Black Bull, Rimington or vice versa.

Clitheroe/Burnley "Betty's Bus", Nos. 201, 202, 203 to the Barley Mow.

Car park/picnic site (map reference 823403).

Map O.S. 2½in. Pathfinder series sheet SD 84/94.

BARLEY is a popular village dominated by Pendle Hill, and the natural instinct of most walkers is to head for the summit of this renowned hill. But below Pendle there are becks and moors which combine to make excellent rambling country, as this walk will show.

Barley to Four Lane Ends: Take the path from the car park that goes behind the toilets and over a footbridge, then turn right to join the road via the children's park. Both car and bus travellers take the road past the Barley Mow to join a rough road on the right, where the road bends left. Around a bend, cross Black Moss Water and a stile on the left which enables you to follow this brook until a small gate leads onto a track. Re-cross the brook here then turn right through a tiny gate and pass by a cottage on the left and a barn on the right.

In the field beyond, follow the trace of a track that goes uphill and turns left alongside a wall. In the corner, pass through a kissing gate and turn left to enter another field at a gap, then turn right to follow the field boundary uphill through two fields, heading for the steep end of Pendle Hill. An overgrown track leads on to reach "Windy Harbour".

Turn left to a stiled gateway on the right after passing the house and gardens, then keep to a right-hand wall over a long field with an open view of Pendle on your left. After a stile continue ahead over an open field which gradually tapers and join the road at a stile by an old gateway near the end. As you go along to the right to reach Four Lane Ends, Ingleborough is ahead with Pen-y-ghent to its right.

For the shorter version: Go right for ¾ mile to a gate on the right where the road bends left. Follow a left-hand wall before bearing right through a gateway by a stream called Water Gate. A track develops and fords the stream to reach "Salt Pie", so named because a heap of salt used to be left here for the use of the local community to preserve food. Fork right at this place and follow the track past Foot House Gate and between two reservoirs (the higher one cannot be seen) to reach a junction. Turn right to reach Barley.

Four Lane Ends to Twiston Mill: For the long version, keep straight

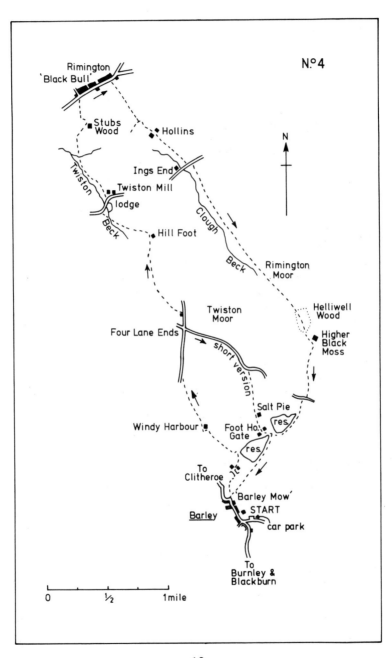

ahead at Four Lane Ends, past some cottages at the foot of the hill to cross a stile on the left, by a gate. Pass through a gateless gap in the wall ahead then bear right to cross another wall at a gap 20 yards from a stream on your left. As you go forward you will see a stile that gives access to a well, but pass it by to cross a stile in a corner.

Pendle stands out boldly on the left as you go down a sloping field to pass to the left of a building. Keep to the lower line of old hawthorn trees on the right, then, after passing a remnant of wall, cross a stile on an external field boundary. A fence on the left leads to a stiled gateway beyond which, the boundary (now on your right) bends right to a gateway in a wall. Sixty yards through this, cross a stiled gate on the left, then bear right very slightly to a stiled gateway below Hill Foot Farm.

Twiston Beck is down to your left as you go forward and gradually descend to reach a stile about 40 yards from the beck after over ¼ mile. Pass between beck and barn then cross the beck at a footbridge after 100 yards. Enter the field to the right to find another gateway just ahead onto the road, but the actual right of way joins the road at a gate higher up the hill.

Twiston Mill to Rimington: Follow the road to the right, then leave (after it bends right) at a stile on the left. Close by is Twiston Cotton Mill which was operated by a waterwheel; activities were terminated by a fire at the end of the 19th century. It has always been owned by the Assheton family of Downham Hall.

Twiston Beck is on your left again and you follow it through five fields. Ignore a footbridge halfway along the fifth field but cross another footbridge at the end, over Ings Beck. Climb the hillside ahead in the direction the footbridge points, to join a right-hand line of trees that leads to a stile on the left-hand side of two gateways. The line of the Roman road between Ribchester and York crosses the route at this point.

Cross the stile mentioned and go alongside the right-hand boundary at first, then bear left to join the access road at a stile at the foot of the hill. (The map seems to indicate that the section of route just described should go through the enclosure of "Stubs Wood", the house you have just bypassed, but at the time of writing, fences blocked the route). To the left by a gate, there is a stile from which you climb up to a gap in the far right-hand corner, then continue in the same direction to join the road at Rimington at a stile. (This stile is near the far corner, but is difficult to see).

Francis Duckworth, who lived at Rimington, named his best known hymn tune after the village; it is used for "Jesus Shall Reign".

Rimington to Rimington Moor: Turn right and walk through the village for about ⅓rd mile to a small gate on the right, opposite "The Old Manor House". In the field, go forward to pass by a group of three trees, after which, keep forward with perhaps an electrified fence to follow. Take note of the permanent field boundary which is parallel, over to the left. Well up the field, it bends right then bends away in the direction you are walking. Between these bends there is a stile (difficult to see) with a stone slab beyond. Over these, keep parallel to the right-hand boundary to cross a stile indicated by some stone stoops, but do not cross the stile just beyond. Instead, follow the tree-lined track to the left; this bends right around a barn and leads on to reach the access road at Hollins, via two stiled gateways.

Another stiled gateway is the start of a climb up an unfenced track to a stiled gate at the top of the rise. For the next ¼ mile there is a left-hand fence to follow, with Ings Beck down to your right, until you join the road near Ings End.

Evidence of lead-mining in this vicinity is a reminder of the time when Sir William Pudsay of Bolton Hall (demolished), near Bolton-by-Bowland, came here and extracted silver from the lead to make counterfeit shillings.

Along the road to the left after 100 yards there is a stile on the right in a short section of a wall. Aim very slightly right, downhill, to cross a footbridge then bear left as you climb a reedy field to cross a line of small trees, so that you have a boundary on the right to follow. This boundary will be your guide for one mile, during which the route will gradually climb through several fields, with Clough Beck over to the right. After you have crossed three wall-stiles, pick your way forward over rough reedy ground (but less steep) to come alongside and follow the right-hand wall seen ahead. This wall divides Rimington Moor on the left, from Twiston Moor on right.

Rimington Moor to Barley: Helliwell Wood comes into view as the way starts to descend and a prominent step-ladder stile gives access into this dark, forbidding plantation. You should be able to walk directly through, but when you reach a clearing, the way ahead is so dense, you will have to bear left to reach another clearing before you can continue forward. After crossing a small stream, the trees are in lines which enable you to have a fairly clear route to emerge at a gateway.

From this, a wall on the left leads to Higher Black Moss where you cross a concrete slab bridge - the most easterly point in this book. Turn right along a track but do not follow it through a gateway into a field, instead keep forward alongside a left-hand wall. Then, when the wall bends left, bear half-left to a stile (difficult to see) on the left of a gate. There is a stream and an embankment on the right as you continue to join a rough road which leads to the public road. A stiled gateway on the far side marks the start of a track that leads past a reservoir. At a junction, turn left to pass another reservoir and continue to reach Barley.

5   A Splendid Track

Hurst Green via Longridge Fell: 8 miles.
Short version via Green Gore: 2½ miles.
Preston - Clitheroe bus service No.9 to Shireburn Arms. (map reference 685379). Parking in village. Maps O.S. 2½in. Sheets SD 63/73 (Pathfinder series) and No.64.

FROM Hurst Green a track heads northwards through the inviting Dean Brook valley. In the open country, beyond the intriguing old house of Green Gore, the track becomes more primitive and it is a joy to the true rambler. Although the character of the walk changes after this, it is ideal rambling country throughout.

Hurst Green to Green Gore: Shireburn Arms is opposite Avenue Road which leads up through the village to the entrance of Stonyhurst College grounds. Notice the Shireburn Alms Houses on the right, which were originally built in 1706 at a site 1½ miles north of the village and rebuilt here in 1947.

Turn left just before the entrance along a track, and fork right near the start, then left, along a narrower path into Mill Wood. Gradually the path descends to come alongside Dean Brook, which you cross on reaching Sandy Bridge. An enclosed sunken track leads away, but the first section of this is so wild that most people clamber over an area of exposed tree roots, to join the track 100 yards further on at a broken section of wall on the left. Negotiate the next section of track which very often becomes water-logged, to reach a junction, with Green Gore about 200 yards ahead.

Green Gore to Hurst Green: For the **short** version, turn left and follow the farm road for about ⅔rd mile to reach Shire Lane and again turn left; this leads back to Hurst Green.

Green Gore to Longridge Fell: For the **long** version, keep straight on to pass Green Gore, about which there is much speculation as to its age (believed to be part 15th century) and history. Once clear of the house, the route becomes wild again, but a wall on the right will guide you to Cronshaw House with a view on your right of Cronshaw Lodge (small reservoir) and Pendle Hill beyond. The route now is along the access road past Holly Hall and uphill to Old Clitheroe Road.

About 80 yards to the right there is a gate on the far side of the road, through which there is a stiled fenced to cross. Now follow a heather-lined path through a plantation for more than ¼ mile to reach a stile leading into the corner of a field.

The correct way from here is up to Green Thorn Farm, seen ahead, then to the right of it to join the path in the plantation beyond. This

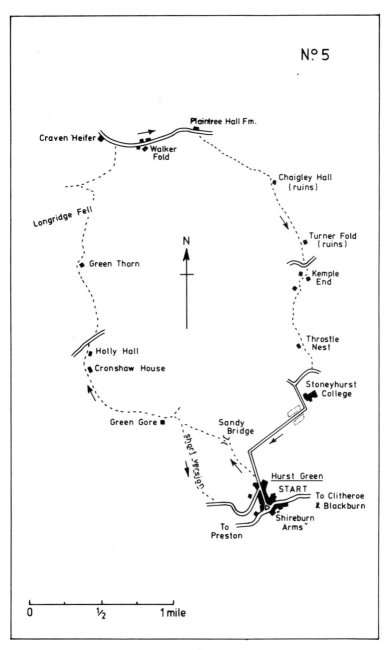

N° 5

Craven Heifer
Plaintree Hall Fm.
Walker Fold
Chaigley Hall (ruins)
Longridge Fell
Turner Fold (ruins)
Green Thorn
N
Kemple End
Throstle Nest
Holly Hall
Cronshaw House
Stoneyhurst College
Green Gore
Sandy Bridge
Hurst Green
START
To Clitheroe & Blackburn
To Preston
Shireburn Arms"

0   ½   1 mile

route has been obstructed for many years by forestry planting and the alternative adopted, although not officially sanctioned, is as follows.

Instead of entering the field at the stile, the alternative keeps inside the plantation with the field on the right. When it has passed the point opposite the farm, the path bears right, behind the farm, then bears left and climbs through the plantation to reach a forestry access road. Cross directly to continue uphill by a similar path that may be obscured in summer by heather and ferns. On reaching another forestry road at the top of Longridge Fell, cross over to a rough track that bears slightly right through a young section of plantation. Eventually, as the trees grow, they will take away the view of Pendle Hill to the right, and that of the valley below, where a ribbon of trees marks the course of the River Hodder flowing from the Bowland Fells.

Longridge Fell to Walker Fold: Watch for the junction with another track where you turn left, then the route descends and bears left to reach a gated fence. Just before this, take another path that doubles back on the right, to make a more steady descent. Leave the path to cross a stile on the left, then rejoin the path at a stile to the right. After continuing in the same direction for a while, turn left through a gateway and follow the track to join a road at a stiled gateway.

Along to the left is the Craven Heifer, which is conveniently situated halfway along the route of this walk. Standing back on the far side of the road is Barracks Farm; one of the buildings is said to have housed some of Cromwell's soldiers.

Walker Fold to Kemple End: On joining the road, the route is to the right, through the hamlet of Walker Fold. At first glance, the most outstanding feature appears to be the telephone box, but the first house on the right is interesting as it was the old Chaigley Charity School.

After passing the main part of the hamlet, there are three more dwellings spaced out along the road, the last of which is Plaintree Hall Farm. Take the first gate on the right after this and cross a single wire fence on the left. Angle uphill at about 45 degrees from the road to cross a stile (hidden at first) in a wire fence. Continue in the same direction to leave the field by crossing a stream, to join a track beyond a fence. Turn right through a gateway, then follow a boundary to the left through two fields. In the next field, still keeping the same direction, the boundary is on the right. This will bring you to an old tree-lined avenue that leads slightly uphill to the ruins of Chaigley Hall.

Turn right, alongside the ruins, then follow a field boundary that bends left and heads for a plantation. Cross a gateway near the plantation and, after crossing a fence, continue with the plantation on your right. On this section you may be able to make out Clitheroe and its castle on your left front. Another ruin, Turner Fold, marks the start of a track that leads to the road at Birdie Brow, by the old Kemple End Quarries.

Kemple End to Hurst Green: Take care as you cross the road to continue by the track opposite, which winds its way past a variety of dwellings to reach a farm. A length of enclosed track starts here (which is usually in a terrible state, owing to its regular use by cows). In the field at the end, join and follow the left-hand boundary until you reach a stile where the boundary bends left. Keep to the right-hand side of the next field until you reach another stile, then go down the right-hand side of the next field.

A stile in the bottom corner leads onto the access road of Throstles Nest, the farm on your right. This leads forward to the road where you go to the right for over 200 yards to where it bends right. Turn left here, through a large gateway into Stonyhurst College grounds. When opposite the centre of the college, turn right between the large lily ponds along a road that runs straight for ½ mile before bending to lead out of the grounds into Hurst Green.(Stonyhurst, described as the most monumental Elizabethan mansion in the country, was started in 1592 by Sir Richard Shireburn and added to over the years, but in 1794, when it was handed over to the Society of Jesus, it was in a state of disrepair. Since then it has been greatly extended and is said to be the most famous of all Roman Catholic Schools. Amongst its possessions is a library containing priceless books and the table upon which Oliver Cromwell slept, prior to the Battle of Preston in 1648).

6   By Bridge and Ford

Edisford Bridge via Daisy Hill Farm: 9¾ miles.
Preston/Clitheroe Bus service No.9 to Low Moor Church (map reference 732415).
Car park on Clitheroe side of bridge (map reference 728414).
Map O.S. 2½in Sheet SD 74.

IT is fitting that this ramble should start at a bridge, for there are many on the route, which also has several streams to ford. Fortunately, there is a bridge at Brungerley, but Henry VI was less fortunate in 1464 whilst fording the river on horseback; his escape bid was thwarted by the Talbots of Bashall Hall and he ended up in the Tower of London. A touch of history then, on a ramble that starts under the gaze of Clitheroe Castle.

Edisford Bridge to West Bradford: Negotiations are in progress for a more suitable route between   Edisford Bridge and Brungerley Bridge, to serve the "Ribble Way" (a long distance footpath devised by the Ramblers' Association). Until this has been established, use the following.

Turn right from the car park to pass Low Moor Church to reach a stile on the left, 40 yards beyond a garage. Walk along an enclosed path which continues beyond a stile to reach a field. Keep to the left-hand side to leave at a stile, then cross the end of a narrow field. Bear right in the next field to a stile on the far boundary, then keep the same direction to a stile in the corner on the left of a gate. Go around the right-hand sides of the next field to leave at a stiled gateway in the diagonal corner, then bear slightly right to reach the River Ribble bank.

As you follow the river to the right, there is a view of Waddow Hall, well known to Girl Guide campers. In the grounds on the river bank, in a small fenced enclosure, you will see Peg O'Nell's headless statue. Peg, a servant in the hall, died following a curse from her mistress. One theory is that the statue came from Whalley Abbey.

Some stone steps lead to the road at Brungerley Bridge, which you cross to enter what was Yorkshire before 1974. Leave the road at a gated track on the right, then keep right at Brungerley Farm, and climb between bushes. At the top, follow the field boundary to the left, then, beyond a stile, descend forward to cross Waddington Brook at a concrete slab bridge. A tributary of this brook is on your right as you go forward over a stile on the right, then cross the tributary at a gateway and another concrete slab.

Leave the next field on the far side at a stile and stone slab (a rutted track flanked by fences, cuts across this field, but there are gaps to allow passage). Avoiding the worn path that goes ahead, bear left to cross the next two fields diagonally (enter the second field at a white gate in the dividing fence) and leave at a stile to the left of the corner. Follow a left-hand hedge to a gateway, through which follow a hedge around to the right to reach a kissing gate in a corner. Keep forward to join a right-hand hedge that leads to a gap stile in a corner, then go left to join the road at West Bradford.

West Bradford to Daisy Hill Farm: Follow the road uphill to the first turning on the right after the Three Millstones. Porter's Brook is down to the right of this track, which turns left at an old Wesleyan churchyard to reach Moor Lane. Turn right and after about 50 yards, just before the entrance to Eaves Hall grounds, there is a signposted path up some steps on the left, to a small wooden gate. Follow the fence enclosing the wooded area on the right, go through a kissing gate, then, where the fence angles to the right, keep ahead to a plank and stile concealed in a dip. Leave the next field at a stile in the far right-hand corner and go through the kissing gate gate beyond. Climb a sloping field towards two renovated buildings (dwellings), following a shallow depression, then pass between these buildings to reach a gate at the left-hand end of a wall.

Dovesyke Farm is two fields away, backed by Waddington Fell. Leave the first field at a gate 40 yards to the right of a cable post, then aim to the right of the farm buildings to join a track beyond a sheep-wire fence. Turn left to pass through a gateway at the far end of the house then bear right to a gate in a fence. Gradually climb, with a wooded stream on the left and continue alongside the stream in the next field. Notice that at first there is a fence between you and the stream, but then the fence crosses to the other side. About 100 yards after the changeover, jump the stream to a stile in the fence where another fence intersects. Aim diagonally to join a track on the right-hand side of Cuttock Clough Farm, then turn left through the yard and follow the access road to Mill Farm. This farm is a reminder of Waddington Corn Mill which was just below the farm by Waddington Brook; further downstream was Feazer Spinning Mill.

The farm road that brought you to this farm continues until it reaches the Clitheroe-Newton road where you continue by the stile opposite. Bear slightly right to a small concrete structure that marks the site of Rushy Well. Stiles enable you to cross the flanking fences and you leave the field beyond, at gateway in the far right-hand corner. Bear right to cross a bridged stream to reach a stile in the far right-hand corner (formed by a stream). Follow a left-hand fence to a stile to the right of the next corner, then go forward to enter Daisy Hill farmyard at a gateway.

Daisy Hill Farm to Saddle Bridge: Pass by the house and turn right at the far end of the buildings, then turn left through the left-hand of two gateways. Beacon Fell and Parlick are ahead and Longridge Fell on the left front as you go alongside a right-hand fence. Leave the next field in the diagonal corner after going around the right-hand sides. Buckstall Farm is on your left, but take the second gate on the right and keep to the right-hand side of three fields to reach the ruins of Burbles Hill Farm, hidden at first, on the right-hand side of a small plantation.

After walking forward to pass the ruins, follow a left-hand fence, but when it bends away, bear half-left to reach the far boundary where it changes from a fence to a hedge. Ford a stream here, to a stile, then continue in the same diagonal direction to a stile on the far boundary 30 yards to the left of where some overhead cables cross the boundary. Ford another stream, then go through a gateway on the right of a barn at Braddup Farm. Go forward and turn left at the house, then go through the first gateway on the right. Take a diagonal route downhill, keeping to the right of overhead cables, to reach Bashall Brook. Follow this to the left to reach the road beyond a stile.

Local residents have assisted nature to make this a very pleasant spot. A walk across Talbot Bridge is worthwhile, before setting off uphill to the left, to a stile up the right-hand bank at the end of a wooded section. Turn right alongside the fenced off wooded brook, to reach a gateway to the left of the corner. Through this, a line of trees lead you downhill to join a track at a wicket gate, with a larger gate nearby. To your right is Clough Bottom Farm, but go left, alongside Bashall Brook, keeping to it when you enter a field.

Here you will come upon the delightful Saddle Bridge (rebuilt 1938) which lies on the old route between Browsholme Hall (1¾ miles over the bridge) and Bashall Hall (one mile further along this ramble route). It has been suggested that it may have served to link the Roman road going north over Marl Hill with the Roman road that passed between Clitheroe and Pendle Hill on its way to York. Another name is Fairy Bridge, because it is said to have been put there by fairies in order to help a kind old woodcutter who was being pursued by witches; the fairies knew that witches would not cross running water.

Saddle Bridge to Edisford Bridge: Do not cross the bridge but continue alongside the brook until it bends away, then keep to the left of some hawthorns which line an unusable sunken track. When you come to where the track is flooded and bears left through a gateway you have to cross to enter the field on the far side at a stile. Follow a fence to the left to reach Cow Hey Farm, where you turn left in the yard, then right, to follow the farm road to reach Bashall Hall.

Notice the first building on the right which was the barracks for the Talbot's private army, with stables underneath. Worthy of attention also is the ancient garden wall which screens the wonderful 16th

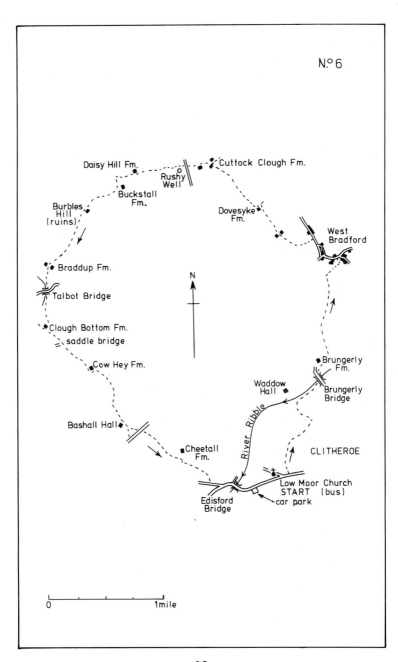

Daisy Hill Fm.
Cuttock Clough Fm.
Rushy Well
Buckstall Fm.
Burbles Hill (ruins)
Dovesyke Fm.
West Bradford
Braddup Fm.
Talbot Bridge
Clough Bottom Fm.
saddle bridge
Cow Hey Fm.
N
Brungerly Fm.
Waddow Hall
Brungerly Bridge
Bashall Hall
River Ribble
Cheetall Fm.
CLITHEROE
Low Moor Church
START (bus)
car park
Edisford Bridge

0   1mile

29

century house. The present occupier is to be praised for extensive tree planting, his contribution to countryside conservation.

Just before the wall ends, go through a gateway on the left and bear right, uphill to join the road at a rail 40 yards to the left of a large sycamore tree. From the stiled gateway opposite, descend through a line of trees to cross a stile on the left of a gate, then turn slightly to the right and cross the field to a footbridge in the far boundary, near to where the remnants of an old hedge meet the boundary. Climb to a stile in the right-hand fence, then follow this boundary to the left to join the main farm road of Cheetall (on your left) at a gate. Cross a stile a short way to the right on the left-hand side, then keep to the right-hand side of this field. Over the stile in the corner, keep forward until you have passed to the right of a small wood, then bear right to join the road at a rail in the field corner. Turn left and left again to descend to cross Edisford Bridge.

7   Old Nick and His Fiends

Fell Foot, near Chipping, via Langden Brook: 15 miles.
Short version finishing at Dunsop Bridge: 10½ miles.
Park in layby at road junction S.E. of Fell Foot (map reference 602442).
Bus travellers will have to start from Chipping (service No.10 from Preston).
This makes the walk 16½ miles and the short version 12 miles (return from Dunsop Bridge by Leedhams Slaidburn - Clitheroe bus service).
Maps O.S. 2½ in Sheets SD 44/54, 65/75 (Pathfinder series) and 55, 64.

"OLD NICK" and his Fiendsdale accomplices must have seemed very real when superstition was rife, for even today one can imagine the Devil still visits Bowland. Wearing his weather mantle he brings rain clouds driven by fierce winds, against which you must wear your waterproof armour and be prepared for swollen streams; take map and compass to outwit his swirling mists. Best to choose a day when "Old Nick's Chair" is empty and the sun transforms the fells into an enchanting wonderland.

Part of the route is over "Access Agreement" land where dogs are not allowed.

Chipping to Fell Foot: At the bus terminus, consult the church weather vane and set off northwards. Fork left at the first and second junctions, right at the third and straight through at the fourth, to reach the buildings at Fell Foot, with Parlick's steep slope directly ahead. This is a popular venue for hang-gliding enthusiasts.

Car travellers take the road northwestwards from the layby to reach Fell Foot.

Fell Foot to Fairsnape: After going through the gateway between the buildings, climb a short steep slope to reach a track. From here you can scramble directly up Parlick, or turn left along this track (once used for bringing down peat-laden sledges) for a much easier ascent. As you climb, Beacon Fell with is plantations becomes prominent on the left front. When you are within 50 yards of a fence, the track elbows back to the right and passes above Fell Foot. Keeping a fairly level route, it then contours around the summit of Parlick, with new views opening out, to reach a junction of walls and fence. This fence is the one that those who have been to Parlick's summit will follow down to reach this spot.

31

Walkers have free access to the land west of the fence and both sides of the wall that continues northwards along the ridge between Parlick and Fairsnape. Stiles enable you to choose which side of the wall to walk, as you follow the ridge to reach another stile after 400 yards. Opposite this is the site of "Nick's Chair" which is generally believed to have been a large cairn, but I cannot help but think that the inspiration for the name came from a small hollow about 40 yards before the stile and just below the top of the escarpment. Sat in this hollow "Old Nick" would be surprisingly sheltered from the wind - try it.

As you look down into the "bowl" of Bleasdale from this spot, you will see Foster's Wood at the foot of the fell. In line with this but further away is Higher Fairsnape Farm and beyond, still in line, is the small wood that shelters the site of "Bleasdale Circle", a "Wood-henge" thought to be about 3,000 years old.

Continue alongside the wall, but be ready for a faint track that gradually bears left and leads to Fairsnape summit (1674ft), crowned with two cairns, a trig. point and useful wind shelter. Given a clear day the view is excellent: Lancashire's entire coastline, Lake District mountains and the Yorkshire peaks of Ingleborough, Whernside and Pen-y-ghent.

Fairsnape to Langden Castle: On leaving the summit you soon encounter the peat hags that are a feature of these fells. Your direction is east-wards so that you can regain the boundary you left (now a fence), near where it changes direction from N.W. to N.E. When the fence changes direction to E.S.E. after ¼ mile, leave it to reach a cairn topped by a post, a short distance to the north.

The next mile of the walk roughly follows the pre-1974 Lanca-shire/Yorkshire border. A short line of stones indicates that you set off from the cairn in a northerly direction but after 100 yards veer N.N.W. At first because of the peaty conditions a worn path has not been established, but small cairns erected by L.L.C. wardens help to keep you on the route until the way becomes grassy and there is a faint worn path to follow. After gradually descending most of the way, the route rises a little as it bears N.W. and you are back amongst the peat hags.

Look out for the "Langden Track" that climbs out of Bleasdale "Bowl" on the left and crosses your route. A post to your left will help identify the track, and upon reaching it you are at the most westerly point in this book. As you follow the track to the right it becomes more pronounced and descends into steep-sided Fiendsdale, with Fiendsdale Water down to your right. Eventually, when the path reaches the valley floor, you must ford Langden Brook which comes in from the left. After also fording a tributary, follow the way-marked route that climbs a little as it goes down the valley to join a track. Go right to

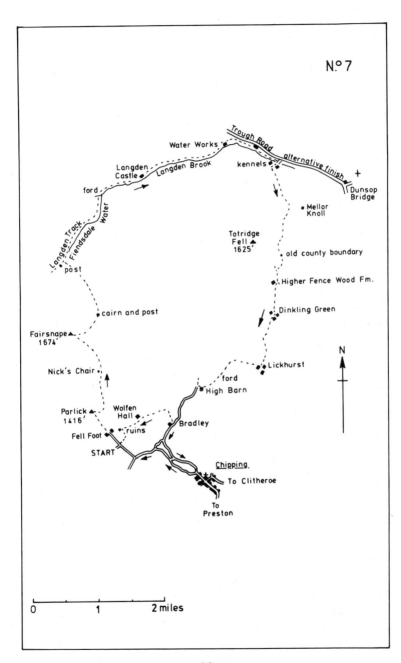

Water Works

Trough Road

Langden Castle

Langden Brook

alternative finish

kennels

ford

Dunsop Bridge

Langden Track

Fiendsdale Water

Mellor Knoll

Totridge Fell 1625′

old county boundary

post

Higher Fence Wood Fm.

cairn and post

Dinkling Green

Fairsnape 1674′

Nick's Chair

Lickhurst

ford

High Barn

N

Parlick 1416′

Wolfen Hall

Bradley

Fell Foot

ruins

START

Chipping

To Clitheroe

To Preston

0   1   2 miles

33

reach the well-concealed Langden Castle, a small stone building that has never been a castle.

Langden Castle to Old County Boundary: Follow the track down the valley (keep right at a junction) for 1½ miles to reach the "Trough" road beyond the waterworks buildings. Your way is to the right and you can either keep to the road or follow a rough route alongside Langden Brook. When a fence intervenes, climb the bank to cross the fence at a stile, then descend to pass below Smelt Mill Cottages and continue until you reach a bridge over the brook.

For those finishing at Dunsop Bridge, continue along the "Trough" road for another mile, then turn left into the village.

For Fell Foot and Chipping, cross the bridge to reach Hareden Kennels after turning right over Hareden Brook. After re-crossing the brook, cross a stiled gateway on the left and climb the hillside to reach a stiled gateway in the left-hand wall. Ignore a track as you turn right and climb steadily with a wall over to your right. Waymark posts will guide you uphill (bypassing two gateways in the wall) until you pass through a gateway in a right-hand corner, with Mellor Knoll summit ahead, and the grandeur of Bowland all around.

A rutted track leads forward, but when it forks into several directions, bear right and aim for the left-hand side of Totridge, the most prominent hill. Waymark posts indicate the route, which is S.W. to reach a gateway in a wall with Hodder Valley now in view on the left. Go forward, closing in on the left-hand boundary, until you are able to cross it at a stiled gateway. A track angles down and up a wooded bank before levelling out for a while, then climbs with the woodland on its left to reach a stiled hurdle in a fence that marks the old county boundary.

Old County Boundary to High Barn: Follow a firebreak straight through a plantation to leave at a gate. Ahead are some hen cabins, where you turn left along a track, then turn right to Higher Fence Wood Farm. Pass the house then, after a gate, turn left in the yard to join a track that leads down to Dinkling Green Brook. Over a footbridge, bear left and cross the fence on the right when you reach a stile. Bear left across a field corner to a stile in a fence, then go forward to enter Dinkling Green farmyard at a gate.

As you go down the yard, notice the mysterious carved face on the left looking across at the date 1774 on the right. At one time there was a school here and the tradition has been revived, because L.C.C. now instruct students here in hill farming.

Turn right after the dated building, through a gateway and follow a track over a ford. Fork left, then left again along a track that dips, then rises, to enter a field where you keep to the right-hand side. In the next field there is a barn ahead, but turn left before this, through a gateway where the left-hand fence bends away. Keep to the right-hand boundary, then after a gateless gap, go through another gateless gap ahead on the right. Pass a small limestone summit on your left as you aim for Lickhurst Farm across a small valley. A stiled fence comes into view down the hill, then join the road below at a footbridge to the right. Lickhurst Farm (refreshments available) is up to the right and here you keep forward to a gate that marks the start of the "Stanley Track", which takes the route on another 1¼ miles. In places the track acts more as a guide than a useable route, but the only directions needed are - fork right through a gateway near the start, ignore a right turn, keep left at another fork. After passing its highest point the track descends to ford Burnside Brook and you turn left when you reach the road beyond the isolated High Barn.

High Barn to Chipping or Fell Foot: For Chipping, follow the road for a good two miles, keeping forward at two junctions.

For Fell Foot, watch out for an isolated barn (Bradley) near the road (after ¾ mile) in a field on the right. Enter this extensive reedy field at a gate and go forward to reach the furthermost boundary before turning left to leave at a gate in the corner. Bear right and descend to cross Chipping Brook at a footbridge by a right-hand fence. At the top of the path that inclines right, pass through a gateway and proceed towards the buildings ahead. There is a fence on your left which you cross at either a gate or stile, to continue with the fence on your right.

Beyond a hurdle is Wolfen Hall where you enter the yard and turn left past the house, then continue forward along a farm road. Leave this before it crosses a cattle grid at gateway 50 yards to the right. Leave a sloping field at a gateway in the far right-hand corner then go forward to the remains of Wildcock House. Turn left along a reedy route to rejoin the farm road and follow it to the right to reach the layby.

8   No Need To Climb A Mountain

Whitewell via Rough Skye Barn: 10¼ miles.
Short version, finish at Newton: 5 miles.
Leedham's Clitheroe/Slaidburn bus service to the Whitewell Hotel
(same service if returning from Newton).
Parking by the church (adjacent to Whitewell Hotel). Map reference
659469.
Can also be started by car or bus at Burholme Bridge (658479) or
Dunsop Bridge (660501).
Maps O.S. 2½ in. sheets SD 65/75 (Pathfinder series) and 64.

WHITEWELL is surrounded by a mixture of limestone hills and
reedy moors, between which runs the beautiful River Hodder. Car
and coach travellers appreciate the area, but ramblers can seek out
places unknown to road travellers and discover that there is no need to
climb a mountain to get a good view.

Whitewell to Higher Birkett: Opposite Whitewell Hotel is the Cow
Ark road and up this on the right hand side are - the old Sunday
School, a flight of stone steps, an access road and another flight of
stone steps. From the small gate at the top of the steps, make for the
right-hand side of Seed Hill cottage ahead and turn left along the far
side of it. Put a line of trees on your right as you climb gradually along
the trace of a track. Beyond a gateway, the track leads onto a
limestone hill, but skirt around the left-hand side of this to rejoin the
road at a gate.

A gated green track opposite continues the route, but when it starts
to descend, make for a step-ladder stile over a wall up to the right.
Turn left to bypass Raven Scar Plantation and pass to the left of a
copse seen ahead (site of a pothole). Continue to climb between two
shallow reedy gullies, then bear right to enter a plantation at a wall-
stile near a fire-beater post.

Follow a fire-break until you reach a stile at the start of a field on the
left. Turn right, but bear away from the right-hand fence, to cross a
broken wall less than 100 yards from the right-hand corner. Ford the
stream just beyond, then cross another wall at a gap guarded by a
corrugated iron sheet. A right-hand fence leads down to Crimpton
Farm where you turn up through the yard and follow the access road
to reach Marl Hill road, which is on the line of the Roman road that
came from Ribchester.

Climb to the left to a gate on the left (the first of two almost adjacent
gates) at the end of the first field beyond Marl Hill Farm. Follow a
right-hand wall to the bottom corner of the field, crossing a fence on
the way. Before you, lies an extensive, rough, ankle-twisting, reedy
area, so take your time to descend, bearing right a little towards

Crimpton Brook. Look across the valley to your right; you will see a wall forming an external corner (your objective) once the brook has been forded. Through a gateway on the corner there is a wall on the left at first, as you gradually descend towards Higher Birkett Farm which comes into view. At the bottom of the hill, ford a tributary of Crimpton Brook and climb a track up to the farm.

Higher Birkett to Rough Skye Barn: In the yard, take the left-hand route along a short length of track into a field. Follow a right-hand wall at first then keep forward across a sloping field, along the trace of a track, to pass above a large hollow and cross a fence where it meets a wall just above Birkett Brook (if unable to cross the fence follow the wall along to a gateway around a corner).

Knowlmere Manor is away to the left, but your way is across Birkett Brook at Giddy Bridge on your right and along the drive, keeping left at a junction. After you have gone through a gateway, leave the drive at the first gateway on the left, then bear right to cross the River Hodder at a suspended footbridge. Bear left towards the right-hand side of the aptly named Knoll Wood to cross a stile by a waterman's gate. Keep the same direction to join the road at gate that serves a track.

Newton is one mile to the right, but for the full walk, enter the field opposite at a stiled gateway, then go forward to reach Forbes Plantation, a narrow belt of trees. On the far side there is a track which, at one time, was part of the main road to Newton. To the left it fords a stream, but your way is forward through a gateway. Keep the stream on your left to reach the access road to "Heaning", the house to your left. Climb the stile opposite, then cross a reedy waterlogged area to come alongside a left-hand line of trees (not edge of wood further to left), which lead uphill to a corner. Go through a gap on the left so that you can continue with the line of trees on your left, to reach the top of the hill, a mere 650ft, but what a splendid view.

Twenty yards to the right of the corner a stone stoop marks the site of the old wall stile. After devising a way to cross, keep to the left-hand wall to cross a wall stile onto Back Lane. Immediately over the stile there is a gate on the left with a stile in it and from this you make to a stile in the diagonal corner. Follow a fence/wall then turn left after passing some barns to enter Gamble Hole farmyard.

As you go up the yard, a barn faces you; pass to the right of this to go through the largest of two gateways. Inside the field there is a very large hole on your right, which is said to have acted as an amphitheatre for cock-fighting, thus giving the farm its name. This field is pitted with smaller holes and there is an interesting theory that they were once much deeper and were made by the Romans in their quest for lead: Gamble Hole Farm is on the line of the Roman road coming north from Ribchester.

This is a very extensive field for it is ½ mile to the far diagonal corner where you leave at a small gateway. This leads onto Bull Lane, a walled grass track which you follow forward, then around a bend to a gateway. Here the track becomes open as it bears right, downhill, to a gateway from where you are looking into the Trough of Bowland, guarded by its sentinels Totridge on the left and Staple Oak Fell.

Rough Skye Barn to Dunsop Bridge: As you descend to Rough Skye Barn, take note of another isolated building (Back of Hill Barn) on the hillside ahead, for this will be your next objective. At the first barn, the track fades but a line of reeds (angling to the right) serves as a link to where the track resumes, as it drops more steeply to Rough Syke running down the attractive Oxenhurst Clough. Over the syke, take the left-hand of the two gates, then ford another branch just beyond. Up the hillside ahead, two fields away, is Back of Hill Barn. Pass through the enclosure on the right-hand side of the barn, then keep forward with a fence on the left, to join a track that bears right, down to Beatrix Farm.

Past the farm the track curves left to pass by a deserted dwelling and a barn. Leave the track when you have passed through a gateway, by crossing a stream on the right, then bear left to keep parallel to the overhead cables on your right. Over a rise, descend into Dunsop Valley to reach a stile in a wood boundary wall about 40 yards to the left of where the cables cross the wall. Immediately over this stile, cross another on the left, descend alongside a fence, then after the foundations of a new building and a stone building, go through a gateway on the right. Pass the rear of Holme Head Cottages then turn left along the access road that leads past Jenny Barn and on to Dunsop Bridge, with the River Dunsop on your right.

Dunsop Bridge to Whitewell: Turn left to pass the post office, Leedsham's garage and public toilets, then turn off through the gateway of Thorneyholme Hotel on your right. Lining the hotel drive are some Californian Redwood trees, identified by their spongy bark. In their native land they attain a height of over 300ft and may be more than 2,000 years old.

Immediately you have crossed the River Hodder, go through a small gate on the right to follow the riverside through four fields. When the river makes a decisive bend to the right, keep forward through two more fields to reach Burholme Farm concealed behind a rise.

High on the wall at the far end of the last barn is the date 1619, one year before the Pilgrim Fathers' sailed. At one time Burholme and Beatrix were hamlets.

Follow the access road to reach Burholme Bridge; do not cross but keep forward to reach Whitewell after less than one mile.

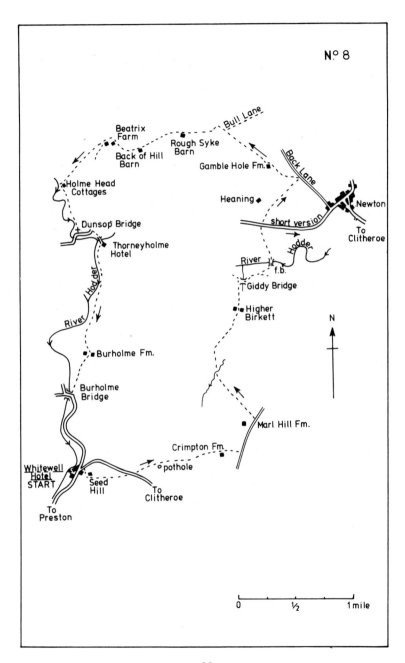

N.º 8

Beatrix Farm
Rough Syke Barn
Back of Hill Barn
Bull Lane
Gamble Hole Fm.
Back Lane
Heaning
Newton
To Clitheroe
short version
Holme Head Cottages
Dunsop Bridge
Thorneyholme Hotel
Hodder
River
River
f.b.
Giddy Bridge
Higher Birkett
Burholme Fm.
Burholme Bridge
Marl Hill Fm.
Crimpton Fm.
pothole
Whitewell Hotel START
Seed Hill
To Clitheroe
To Preston

N

0   ½   1 mile

9   Secluded Charm

Newton via Harrop Fold: 10 miles.
Short version to catch "Betty's Bus" at Landing Lane: 5½ miles.
Limited services - Tues.& Thu. (202); Wed.(204)
Leedham's bus service from Clitheroe to Newton.
Limited parking for cars on the road near the river bridge (map ref. 699502).
Maps O.S. 2½in. Sheets SD 65/75 (Pathfinder series), and 74.

FROM Newton this route climbs steadily onto Grindleton Fell which lies between the Hodder and the Ribble. Harrop Fold is a charming secluded hamlet that heralds the second half of the walk, which, in stark contrast with the section through Grindleton Fell plantation, is of a unique open character.

Newton to "Old Ned": From the village, cross the river Hodder and take a stiled gate on the left. A faint track leads to another stiled gate just beyond a ditch, and as you leave the river keep to the right-hand side of a long narrow field. Leave at the topmost gate, from where a track leads to the road. Over the stile opposite, bear left to cross a stile and stream at a stone slab. From the stone slab gradually climb, closing in on a tree-lined stream on the left, which you cross almost opposite Meanley Farm and climb away, keeping outside an enclosure at first to join the access road. Turn right to pass to the left of the farmhouse, then beyond a small gate, climb with a boundary on your right to pass through a gateway in a corner (a barbed wire fence may intervene). Still climbing, you will soon have a wooded stream on your left with more woodland over to the right. A left-hand fence continues the route to reach an access road beyond a gate.

Go left to pass a farmhouse intriguingly called Smelfthwaites, then turn right after a stone barn to pass through a gate. Keep a stream on your right as you gently climb to a small concrete structure where you bear left along a slightly raised causeway; this sets you off in the right direction over reedy ground to reach a gateway in a stone wall.

Here is an excellent place to turn around and have a rest whilst you admire the view of the Hodder Valley and a wide sweep of fells beyond.

The hillside is steeper beyond the gate and you angle to the right, along a reedy sunken way to meet another sunken way which you follow to the left. A landmark to look out for when the route levels is a small tarn over to the right. Soon the path becomes fainter and fords a small stream at some stepping stones. There is a low rise ahead that marks the top of Easington Fell and you pass over the left-hand slope of this, then keep forward, gradually climbing over trackless ground to

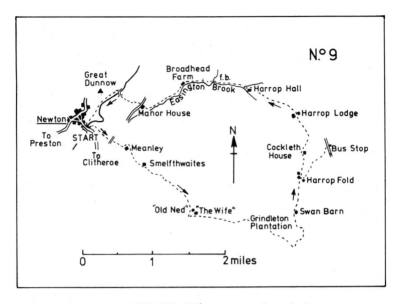

reach a cairn (named "Old Ned") by a rutted track that cuts across your route. At this point the Ribble Valley comes into view and Waddington Fell Quarries are over to the right.

"Old Ned" to Harrop Fold: One hundred and sixty yards beyond "Old Ned" is "The Wife", another cairn, which like "Old Ned" used to be much larger. A short way after this, turn left along a grass track to cross a wall at a step-ladder stile, then keep ahead with Pendle on the right front. Gradually the track descends through a gateless gap, and you pass two shooting butts on your right, to reach a plantation. Cross a stile to the left and rejoin the track which enters a rough pocket of land bordered by trees on three sides. When the track bends left, keep forward to reach a wall gap and concealed stile at the far end of the pocket, near the left-hand corner. This takes you into the plantation on Grindleton Fell which you will not leave for another 1¼ miles.

Continue downhill with a wall on the right, then turn left alongside a broken wall, but after about 50 yards turn right, downhill. After a steep part, a track develops which leads through this plantation to reach a turning area at the end of an access road. On the far side the rutted track bears left a little and fords a stream, but shortly after, turn left alongside a left-hand wall. At a corner, turn to keep the wall on your left, then after 150 yards, turn left through a gap in the wall and follow a left-hand wall to reach the plantation boundary.

At the time of writing, it was intended to make some adjustment to the path to reach Swan Barn seen below to the left. Until stiles are provided proceed as follow. Turn left downhill until you reach a gap a few yards beyond where the plantation boundary wall makes a zig-zag (a wire fence has to be climbed to reach the gap). Descend a sloping field (ignore the step-ladder stile) towards the barn, which has Ingleborough directly above. Enter the next field at a gate on the left of the barn, then keep forward with a stream on the right to leave the field at a gateway. Keep to the left-hand side of the next field until taking the left-hand of a pair of gates, then keep ahead to enter Harrop Fold.

For the short version: Turn right, then left, to follow Landing Lane to the end where you catch Betty's Bus. Along Landing Lane on the left is the oldest Methodist chapel in the Clitheroe area, built 1821.

Harrop Fold to Newton: On your left is the Manor House and you bear left after this to locate a wall stile near the far left-hand corner of a green strip between buildings. Leave an enclosure at a stile and follow a left-hand boundary to leave at the right hand of two gates, then go through a gate on the right near the far diagonal corner to join a track. Turn left along this, then turn left again between the buildings of Cockleth House to enter a field at a wall stile by a dogpen at the back of the house.

Bear half right to the far diagonal corner to reach a track where it bridges a stream by wooden railed pens. Do not cross this stream but cross the track to a gap in a fence just beyond a ditch. Continue alongside a right-hand boundary to join a track and enter Harrop Lodge yard.

Bear right, through a gate, to join the access road where you go right before crossing a rough piece of land on the left, to enter a field at a gate. The next section of the walk, which is straight ahead for more than ½ mile, has in succession a wall, fence and a stream on the right. Finally, beyond a wall stile a left-hand wall leads to an access road, with Harrop Hall to the left.

Your way is to the right, but when it bends right, cross a grass verge on the left to a wall stile and continue with Easington Brook on the left. When a wall intersects the brook, cross a wall stile about 60 yards from the bank, and then a footbridge to the left over Langcliffe Brook. Continue with the main brook on your left and a wall on the right. Beyond a gate the brook leads to Cockshutts Part (now called Broadhead Farm).

Leave the yard at two consecutive gates in the right-hand corner beyond the house. Enter the field ahead at another gate and continue forward to rejoin the brook after it has made an elbow to the left. When a fence intervenes, go through a gateway on the left so that you can continue between fence and stream to reach a track where it bridges the stream - do not cross! After passing a barn, follow the track around to Manor House or take a short cut.

Pass through the yard to reach the road then cross over to a gate just to the left. A left-hand hedge leads to a kissing gate in a corner, through which aim half-right to the left of a group of trees that are backed by Great Dunnow, a steep wooded limestone hill. A kissing gate will come into view in an iron fence and beyond this, a rare iron footbridge points the way to a large bridge across the River Hodder. Sombre looking Dunnow Hall is ahead, but bear left to the sharp end of a field to leave at a kissing gate and continue between the river and hill. Enter the river-side field at the left-hand of two small gates and leave at a wall stile in the far right-hand corner. Beyond a footbridge to the left, a riverside path leads to Newton.

10   Bolton by Beckland

Bolton by Bowland via Stephen Moor: 10 miles.
Short version via Varley's Farm Road: 4¾ miles.
"Betty's Bus" from Clitheroe (Wednesday only) will allow 5 hours
21 mins. for the walk. Near the end of the ramble, "Betty's Bus" can
be caught at Copy Nook; this will save the last ½ mile walk into
Bolton by Bowland and gain the time that the bus takes to travel
from the village to Copy Nook.
Cars can be parked at the village hall behind the Coach and Horses,
where the bus stops. (Map reference 785493).
Maps O.S. 2½ins. Sheets S.D. 65/75 (Pathfinder series), and 74.

IF possible, allow time to look around this attractive village and include a visit to the church, built about 1464 by Sir Ralph Pudsay. Carved alongside him on a remarkable limestone tomb are his three wives and twenty five children.

Bolton by Bowland could justifiably be called Bolton by Beckland because of the many becks in the area that converge to enter the nearby River Ribble. Of these Bond Beck is outstanding and contributes to the wide variety of scenery encountered on this walk. No big hills to climb but the views are impressive. Warning! At the time of writing, the long version of this ramble entails fording New Gill Beck, which can be quite adventurous after heavy rain.

Coach and Horses to Lodge Farm: Turn left as you leave the car park along Main Street, to a stile on the right after you have crossed Skirden Bridge. On your right is Skirden Beck, the first and most important of all the becks encountered on this ramble - all the rest run into it. At first the route is alongside the beck but then it climbs above as you follow the stiles and there is a fence on your right. After a small gate, a right-hand line of trees leads to a similar gate with stone steps. Join the road at a gate on the left front then go right for 500 yards to a gate on the left as you reach Stoop Lane Farm dated 1703.

Bear right to reach Green Ford Farm over the crown of the hill. A stone wall stile towards the left-hand end of the buildings leads into the enclosure where you bear right to pass around a Dutch barn. Turn left to a stone barn which faces a green gate across the yard on the right-hand side of a silage heap. In the field, cross Cuddy Syke at a concrete bridge on the left front, then angle away from the stream to cross a stile in the far corner and ford a tributary. Turn left to cross a stile in the corner, then aim up to Newhurst Farm. Enter the yard and turn right, past the house front then along the access road to reach a minor road.

For the short version turn left and follow for over ¼ mile to pass a cottage on the right (Broad Ing) to reach a sharp bend where the farm road to Varley's keeps forward over a cattle grid. Over this, turn sharp left and continue as described in section headed "Varley's Farm road to Bolton by Bowland".

For the main route cross straight over the minor road to follow the farm road to Wittons Farm (formerly Higher Wittons 1704). Keep ahead through the yard to enter a field at a gate on the left of a large building. Bear right after this building to pass through a gateway leading into a sloping reedy field where you turn left and gradually angle away from the left-hand boundary to pass through a line of trees. Continue to the right of a slight ridge to reach a gate in a tree-lined fence, about 70 yards to the right of the field corner. Bear right to cross a stony gap in another line of trees,then left to reach the deserted Lodge Farm.

Lodge Farm to Stephen Moor: A small gate immediately in front of this building gives access to the enclosure and you go around the right-hand end to leave at a wall stile. Through a gateway to the right,follow an enclosed track to enter a field. Thirty yards ahead, bear left to ford a small stream then pass over a slight rise to descend a fern-clad hillside to reach a gateway; New Gill Beck is beyond and a tributary on its left. Through the gateway, bear left to cross the beck (beware of slippery rocks) at an angle, to reach the far bank at a short length of sunken track.

Follow the bank to the left to pass the remains of Midge Hall Farm (where a hurdle has to be climbed) to reach Beckfoot Farm (formerly Gills) after ½ mile. Pass through the yard and continue alongside what is now called Bond Beck to reach a footbridge in line with a gated fence. From this point the route is along the other bank. Halfway through the second field a fence starts on the right and you cross it at a rail, after a few yards. Continue alongside the beck through two more fields to reach a field gate.

This brings you to the house "Butter Fields" where a bridge crosses Little Beck (tributary of Bond Beck). Do not cross the bridge but go through the gateway between the bridge and the road going off on the left. Climb with the garden fence on your right at first then follow the fence on the left with Little Beck down to your right. The next section of the walk is over part of Stephen Moor, which introduces another significant change in the character of the walk.

Stephen Moor to Varley's Farm road: After a gated fence there is a wall on the left which divides when you reach a gateway with a wall stile on the right and an old lime kiln over to the left. Use the gate if the stile is too awkward then head for the gap in the wall on the sky-line which comes into view. Gradually, you will close in on the right-hand boundary to leave the field at small gate in the far corner to the left of the gap. Keep forward in the next field with a small stream on your left, to reach a wall stile on the right of a gate. Do not cross, but turn left alongside the wall then alongside a right-hand fence in the next field. After another gate, an enclosed track leads to a small gate opposite the last remaining building of Fells Farm.

Head in the same direction as you climb to the highest point of this ramble (900ft) where you climb a wall stile protected by a gated fence. Pendle Hill is on the left front as you continue down a rough field, gradually closing in on the left-hand wall to join the road at another wall stile. Turn left immediately to follow a track to the unoccupied Ling Hill Farm, in front of which turn right and head straight across a field to reach a rare double-stepped stile. Put a sheep-wire fence on your right as you keep forward through two fields, with Grindleton Fell ahead. Cross a wall stile on the right, almost at the end of the second field, then bear slightly left to a gate on the left of Threap Green Farm and follow a track past the farm and on to the road.

Follow the road to the left for nearly ½ mile to a track on the left where the road bends sharply to the right. Through the gateway ahead, continue with a boundary on the left, passing through another gateway ahead, and crossing two sykes to another gateway. This marks the start of an intriguing pleasant avenue flanked by streams and trees (mostly holly) as well as a holly hedge on the right. Turn right on reaching a minor road and right again at a bend to cross a cattle grid at the start of Varley's farm road.

Varley's farm road to Bolton by Bowland: Turn sharp left over the cattle-grid and head for a gateway, through which follow the right-hand boundary through two fields. Well down the second field, go through a gateway on the right that leads into a field, with a barn nearby. Leave this field at a gate midway in the bottom boundary, then bear right as you go down the next field to discover a plank bridge, to cross Higher Syke on the right. Ascend the track to Wycongill Farm, pass through the yard and follow the access road.

Just before reaching the public road, take a gated track on the left and keep to the left-hand side of one field then descend another to pass to the right of a small stone building. Pass between this building and the house: Hungrill, to cross Hungrill Beck at a gated bridge. Follow the beck to the right to enter a yard by a barn and leave at a gate on the right, to be confronted by a ford and stepping stones; these are said to lie on an old monastic route coming from Sawley Abbey 2½ miles due south.

Re-cross the beck here to follow a track then turn left at a junction. After 60 yards, go through a gateway on the right and follow a right-hand fence at first before curving left around a hillside. For a while keep parallel to a small beck down to your right, before descending to

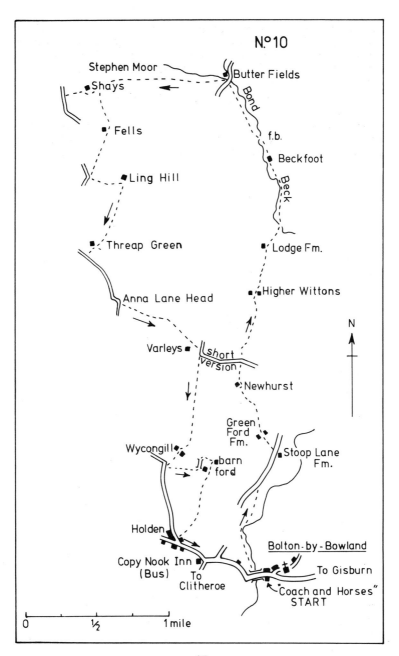

N°10

Stephen Moor

Butter Fields

Shays

Bond

Fells

f.b.

Beckfoot

Ling Hill

Beck

Threap Green

Lodge Fm.

Anna Lane Head

Higher Wittons

N

Varleys short version

Newhurst

Green Ford Fm.

Wycongill

Stoop Lane Fm.

barn ford

Holden

Bolton-by-Bowland

Copy Nook Inn (Bus)

To Gisburn

To Clitheroe

"Coach and Horses" START

0   ½   1 mile

cross it at some stone slabs between two bends. Continue along the other side but when the beck bends away, bear right slightly to leave the field at the very end, at a rail on the left of two double-trunked trees in the field boundary. Follow a left-hand boundary to a gate in the corner, then turn right to join the road at a stile and steps.

To your left is a junction at the pretty hamlet of Holden, where a short walk to the right to stand on the bridge over Mear Gill is worthwhile. Retrace your steps to the junction and follow the road to the next junction at Copy Nook where the bus may be caught. For Bolton by Bowland, turn left here and right at the next junction.

11   A Remote Corner of England

Slaidburn via Lock Bridge: 11½ miles.
Leedham's Clitheroe/Slaidburn bus service.
Carpark near river, (map reference 714523).
Map O.S. 2½ins. Pathfinder series sheet SD 65/75.

IT is not surprising that there is a youth hostel at Slaidburn, for it is surrounded by excellent walking country. There is a remoteness about the area which is illustrated by St. James Church on the eastern shore of Stocks Reservoir. Rebuilt in 1938 from the stones of its predecessor, it stands like a monument to the village of Dalehead (Stocks in Bowland) which lies submerged beneath the reservoir.

Slaidburn to St. James: From the car park walk uphill to the war memorial (where bus passengers alight). Take the Bentham road here, but leave it at a kissing gate on the right when you have crossed the bridge over Croasdale Brook. Follow the brook until it bends away, then bear slightly left along a line where the field shelves, to come alongside a left-hand wall that leads to a gate in the corner. In the next field the wall leads on to a surfaced farm road which crosses Holmehead Bridge on your right, then follow the track to the left alongside the River Hodder. After crossing Barn Gill, the track is enclosed as it climbs to the last building on the right of Hammerton Hall Farm. It is said that in the old days, the Hamerton's (spelt with one 'M') where so dominant, they could ride all the way to York upon their own land.

The track now bends right and climbs a little into an enclosure where you take the left-hand of three gates. A very faint track leads uphill through two fields with a wall on the right and the scant remains of an old boundary on the left. Continue with a plantation fence on the left to reach a corner, where, through the left-hand gateway, the route is between the fence and a wall,. After turning right you will come to a fence, but go through a facing gateway on the right and continue alongside a left-hand wall. Another gate allows you to pass to the right-hand side of a wood to reach Black House Farm. Follow the farm road to the left to reach Hole House Lane, with good views of Stocks Reservoir on the way.

St. James Church to Lock Bridge: Your way is past the church, where (inside) you can read the story of the church and village. Later the road crosses a causeway which cuts across a small inlet of the reservoir, and ⅓rd mile further on where it bends sharply to the right, go through a gateway on the left. On your right is the site of the old church and the site of Stocks in Bowland lies close at hand beneath the water.

The next ¾ mile of the route is through a plantation, proceeding generally in a N.N.W. direction and you should emerge near the northern-most tip of the reservoir. Plantations can be tricky places to negotiate, but here is the description of the route.

Follow a track that bends right then keep right at a fork through a gateway and follow a forest ride. Ignore a turning on the right, climb gently and fork right. After turning right the ride climbs to some ruins where you turn left and keep ahead to reach a small building and more ruins. Turn left again along another ride to finally emerge from the plantation at a kissing gate.

After crossing a reedy area via a green route, cross Hasgill Beck at a bridge on the right and climb steadily alongside a left-hand boundary for ½ mile to reach the ruins of New House. Here the track bears right, then, after a gateway, a green track forks off to the right just around a bend.

It would seem sensible to keep to main track, but the public right-of-way makes a detour up the green track which heads for Pike Side summit. There is no need to go to the top because when you reach a wall, the route you want angles back downhill to rejoin the main track where the wall comes downhill to meet it. Just after this it crosses Parks Clough Beck at a bridge and follows the clough downhill (the most northerly point in the book). When it bends away, leave it to continue alongside the clough to join Catlow Farm access road, which you follow forward over the River Hodder at Lock Bridge.

Lock Bridge to Slaidburn: More than ½ mile further on, beyond Kenibus Farm, is the Slaidburn/High Bentham road where you turn left. After nearly one mile the road reaches the top of a hill with Merrybent Hill Farm set back on the left. Continue along the road for another ½ mile then turn right where the road bends left. This leads to Clough Farm, but leave it to cross the field on the left to reach a gap in a fence to the left of an isolated barn.

Go forward to join a right-hand field boundary along level ground at first, then descending to pass through a gap in a corner. Ahead, across two fields, is another barn (Wood Laithe) which you reach via two stiles. Bear right to follow a right-hand fence downhill through two fields to join the farm road on the left of Croasdale House.

Follow this to the left, turning left and right, past some farm buildings, a few trees and a gateway. Leave the farm road shortly after this to cross a stiled gateway over on the right, then keep forward with Croasdale Brook on your right to join a track at a gate.

Shay House Farm is over the bridge to the right, but cross straight over the track to continue with the brook on your right. When it bends away, bear slightly left to leave the field at a wall stile ahead on the left

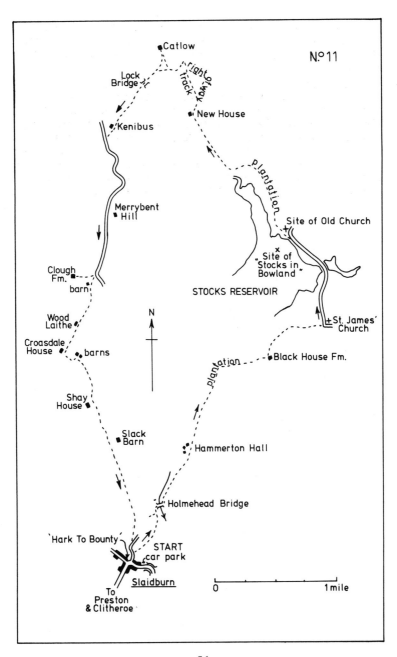

Catlow

Lock Bridge

right of way track

New House

Kenibus

plantation

Merrybent Hill

Site of Old Church

Site of "Stocks in Bowland"

Clough Fm.

barn

STOCKS RESERVOIR

Wood Laithe

N

St. James' Church

Croasdale House

barns

Black House Fm.

Shay House

plantation

Slack Barn

Hammerton Hall

Holmehead Bridge

Hark To Bounty

START car park

Slaidburn

To Preston & Clitheroe

0   1 mile

of a gateway. In the next field, the right-hand boundary bends away but rejoin it near the far end of the field as you climb to leave at a wall stile in the corner. (Slack Barn over to the left is a landmark in this field).

A scant line of hawthorns point the way in the next field to a stile in the wall that crosses the crown of the hill. Keep ahead to cross a stile (not easy to see) in a fence 80 yards to the left of Waterhead Wood, then keep the same direction, aiming to the left of a long narrow belt of trees to leave this field at a wall stile. Leave the next field at another wall stile at the left-hand end of the belt of trees already mentioned, then go downhill, keeping to the right of a wall and a line of trees. Keep forward when this boundary bends away but bear left further down the field to join the road at a stile that is difficult to see. Slaidburn is to your right.

12 Lonely But Wonderful Whitendale

Slaidburn via Whitendale: 13 miles
Short version via Dunsop Head: 7¾ miles.
Leedhams Clitheroe/Slaidburn bus service.
Car park by the river (Map reference 714523).
Maps O.S. 2½ins. Pathfinder series sheet SD 65/75.

IF you want to "get away from it all", take a walk up the Whitendale Valley where the hills close in around, creating a lost world. There is a rare peace and quiet here that you can absorb to your hearts content.

Slaidburn to Dunsop Head: Turn right out of the car park and climb past the war memorial and straight past "Hark to Bounty". After more than a mile, Wood House Lane (cul-de-sac) goes off on the right, but keep on for another 300 yards to join a rough farm road on the right, around a bend. Burnside can be seen half-a-mile away and, after passing to the right of this house, the track continues in a wild and reedy state. Soon it succumbs to the bumpy nature of the ground but a wall on the right acts as a guide as you pick your way to a gateway concealed in a dip 30/40 yards to the left of the corner.

Immediately in front is the steeper slope of Dunsop Fell, but a sunken way that inclines to the right enables you to make a more gradual climb. After about 250 yards this track curves sharply back to the left. Your aim is to climb along a ridge so that you have the lower ground just crossed on your left and the deep-sided valley of Dunsop Brook opening up on your right. Behind, over your left shoulder, can be seen Stocks Reservoir, north of Slaidburn.

From a confusion of tracks, one survives and keeps on or near the top of the ridge at first but then veers to the right, above the top end of the valley. On the top of Dunsop Fell cross a narrow mossy-banked stream and a wall comes in from the left. Gradually close in on this wall to reach a well-concealed small gate at Dunsop Head - a splendid view-point.

Dunsop Head to Slaidburn (short version): Do not go through the gate but walk directly away from it passing to the left of some scattered boulders which suggest an ancient settlement. Ahead the land is heathery on the left, reedy on the right. Keep to the fringe of the heather (look for a waymark post) to approach a fence coming in from the left. This forms a corner with a wall that runs in the direction you are walking. Look over to your right for another waymark post which indicates the start of a faint rutted track. This track is on the opposite side of Dunsop Brook Valley by which you came. It keeps above the valley but gradually descends with Stocks Reservoir ahead to reach a rough road after one mile.

Follow this road to the right for nearly a mile. You will pass Higher Wood House Farm, then in succession on the left there is a farm road, barn and track. Follow the track which fords a stream and climbs a field. At the top of the hill look for a stiled gateway in the wall on the left. This stiled gateway is at the end of the second field after Simfield House, as mentioned in the longer version (second paragraph from end), so do not cross the stile but turn your back to it and cross to the tree-lined boundary to find the wire fence with the barbs removed. Continue as described.

Dunsop Head to the Salter Fell Track (long version): From here to Whitendale Farm (which will remain hidden for some time) the route has been waymarked by the North West Water Authority. Through the gate, a path angles sharply to the right through the heather, with Totridge Fell the most prominent bump to your left. For a while the route is fairly level but then it gradually descends with Middle Knoll ahead between the Whitendale and Brennand valleys. To the left of the knoll, the two rivers unite to form the Dunsop River which flows southwards for two miles to join the River Hodder at Dunsop Bridge.

Whitendale Farm comes into view as you start to descend more steeply and a grouse-shooters' track finally leads down to the farm. Pass through the yard with buildings over to your right, then turn right at a junction to cross a bridged tributary to put the River Whitendale, your companion for the next 1¾ miles, on your left.

A pack of sheepdogs will have announced your presence but you will soon leave these and the farm behind as you follow a riverside track past a bridge (not over) to reach a fork beyond a gateway, where you keep left. The track soon climbs, then fades a little before descending again, but leave it before it descends as you head slightly uphill to a gateway on the right front. After passing between new plantations, the ground becomes very uneven where waymarks are provided in the form of stony stream crossings. Later a more distinct path develops, trodden out more by sheep than by humans one would surmise.

When the path fades away again keep the river as a companion and look out for a cairn (perhaps concealed by ferns in the summer) and ford a stream shortly afterwards. Appropriately, this wild lonely spot marks the halfway mark of the ramble. Leave the river to angle up the hillside that forces the river to change direction; in effect you are still keeping the same direction as before. After a rough and tough climb of ½ mile you will reach Hornby Road, better known as the Salter Fell Track. You will come upon it without much warning for it is primitive and unfenced. Salt was carried along this route by packhorses, but just how long it has existed is not known.

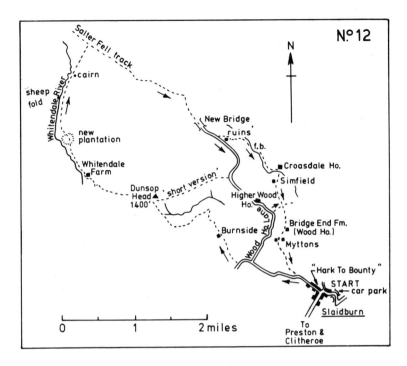

Salter Fell Track to Slaidburn: To the left the track leads to Hornby in the Lune valley, but follow it to the right for two miles, to cross New Bridge. About ¼ mile further on, opposite a small building that stands by Croasdale Brook down to your left, look for a faint track that angles off to the left. This gradually descends down the hillside then contours around to reach the concealed ruins of "The House of Croasdale". Through the gateway, angle down the hillside at the best possible place then follow Croasdale Brook until you are able to cross it at a bridge (about ½ mile beyond the ruins) reached through a gateway. Continue along the other side using a worn path to contour around a hillside, then bear left with a wood on your right, to enter Croasdale House yard after fording Moor Syke.

Pass straight through the yard and follow the access road for about 50 yards before leaving it to cross a gated footbridge on your right which takes you back over Croasdale Brook. Cross a small field and climb through a belt of trees to cross a stile.

At the time of writing the next section entailed climbing three wire fences. One was immediately after the stile, the second on the far side of a small field to enter the enclosure of Simfield house, the third was to leave the enclosure to enter the field which the house front faces. It

55

is hoped that these problems will be sorted out by the time this book is published.

Leave the sloping field in front of Simfield House at a gateway in a wall on the right, near the bottom right-hand corner. There is an access road here but cross a stile on your immediate left in a corner, then bear right over the crown of a field to cross a stiled gateway. On the far tree-lined boundary you will find a section of wire fencing with the barbs removed. Over this, keep to the left-hand side of two fields, then cross a stile that enables you to pass to the right of an isolated barn. Cross a field to Bridge End Farm and go through a small gateway by a brook on the right.

Turn right to cross the brook and pass through a gateway, then cross a stile on your immediate left. Over the next field, another small gate on the right-hand side of Myttons leads to a gate on the right where you enter the yard. On the far side a walled track leads to a field where you follow a wall to the left to leave at a gate in the corner. Bear half-right in the next field to leave at a stone slab bridge and cross the wall stile just beyond. Tree-lined Croasdale Brook is on your left now, but after a stile follow a left-hand fence to rejoin the brook after it has made a loop. A path by a shady section of the brook will lead you to the road where you turn left to retrace the first part of the walk back into Slaidburn.